It's Not Fair

Carol Gorman

Illustrated by Rudy Nappi

CPH ™

SAINT LOUIS

Copyright © 1992 Carol Gorman

Published by Concordia Publishing House
3558 S. Jefferson Avenue, St. Louis, MO 63118-3968
Manufactured in the United States of America

Library of Congress Cataloging-in-Publication Data.

Gorman, Carol
    It's not fair by Carol Gorman: illustrated by Rudy Nappi. (The Tree House Kids)
    Summary: The Tree House Kids are devastated to hear that their friend Kara has leukemia, and they become angry with God.
    ISBN 0-570-04714-5
    [1. Leukemia—Fiction.   2. Christian life—Fiction] I. Nappi, Rudy, ill. II. Title. III. Series: Gorman, Carol. Tree House Kids.

PZ7.G6693It 1992
[Fic]—dc20
                                    91-40592
                                        CIP

2 3 4 5 6 7 8 9 10 11   03 02 01 00 99 98 97 96 95

For my mother-in-law,
Bea Gorman Hixenbaugh,
with love

Series

Contents

Where's Kara?

"Where's Kara?" Tess Munro asked, turning to gaze over the playground.

"Kara LaMasters?" Ben Brophy said. "I don't know. She hasn't been in school all week."

"She must be sick," Roger Quinn said, bending over a book in his lap.

The kids were sitting on the school playground waiting for the first bell to ring. Ben was tossing a softball in the air and catching it. Tess was drawing purple and pink squiggles on her notebook around the words *The Tree House Kids*.

Ben, Tess, and Roger had formed a club recently to figure out what to do about a school bully. Since their meeting place was a tree house in Mrs. Pilkington's backyard,

7

they decided to call their club The Tree House Kids.

Roger was sitting cross-legged in the grass, working on a crossword puzzle from a paperback book.

"I miss Kara too," Roger said. "She likes crossword puzzles as much as I do, and she helps me figure out the hard words."

He frowned. "Can you think of a five-letter word meaning finger or toe?" His face brightened. "I know! *Digit!*" He wrote in the letters. "Kara would've gotten that right away." He grinned. "She's really smart."

"Yeah," Ben said. "She's also a great softball player." He set the ball in the grass and tied his loose shoelace.

"I know," Tess said. "She's the best pitcher we've got. But she hasn't been playing the last couple of weeks. She always says she's tired."

"Let's ask Ms. Conley when we get inside," Ben said. "Maybe she knows what's going on with Kara."

"Okay," Tess said.

"Tell me at lunch what Ms. Conley says," Roger said.

The first bell rang, and the kids lined up

in rows at the front door. Ben and Tess stood in the third-grade line, Roger in the second-grade line.

After they were inside, Ben and Tess hurried to talk to their teacher. Ms. Conley stood in the hallway watching the kids file into the building.

"Hi, Ms. Conley," Ben said.

"Hello, Ben. Hi, Tess," Ms. Conley said.

She smiled. Ms. Conley was a nice teacher, and both Ben and Tess liked her. She was hard, though. She expected her students to do their best work every day.

"We haven't seen Kara LaMasters all week," Ben said. "Is she sick or something?"

"Yes, she is," Ms. Conley said, her smile fading a little. "Her mother called yesterday after school and said that Kara's been feverish and unusually tired the last couple of weeks. She's going to see a doctor today."

"Oh," Tess said. "So maybe the doctor will give her some medicine, and she'll be back next week."

"I hope so," said Ms. Conley. "I've missed having her in class." She paused. "Maybe she just needs a little rest."

"We need her on our softball team," Ben said.

"Well, I hope she'll be back soon," Ms. Conley said.

"Let's call her after school," Tess said to Ben. "You guys can come to my house."

"Okay," Ben said. "Thanks, Ms. Conley."

After school, Ben and Roger walked home with Tess. They tromped up the front steps, and Tess opened the door with her key. The kids walked into the silent house.

"Where's your mom?" Roger asked.

"Probably not home from the hospital yet," Tess said.

"She's in the hospital?" Roger asked.

"Yeah, but she's not a patient. She's a nurse," said Tess. "She works from seven to three, but lots of times she stops at the grocery store or someplace else on the way home."

"Oh," Roger said.

"My sister might be here, though," Tess said. She threw her head back and yelled, *"Ash-ley!"*

"What?" a voice called from upstairs.

"I'm home!" Tess hollered.

"So what?" the voice said.

"So I though you'd want to know," Tess yelled.

"I'm doing my nails," Ashley called.

Tess rolled her eyes. "Of *course* she's doing her nails. She's *always* doing her nails." She turned to Roger. "Ashley's 15," she said. "All she cares about are doing her nails, boys, listening to the radio, boys, hanging out at the mall, boys, and clothes. And did I say boys?"

Ben and Roger laughed.

"Right, Ben?" Tess said.

"Right," Ben said.

Tess made a face. "You won't catch me getting weird like that when I'm 15."

"You won't have to," Ben said, grinning. "You're weird *now*."

"Don't get smart, Ben," Tess said over her shoulder as she headed for the phone in the kitchen. "Let's call Kara."

She picked up the receiver and dialed.

"Hi, Mrs. LaMasters," she said a moment later. "Is Kara there, please? This is Tess Munro."

Ben and Roger stood next to Tess, watching her.

"Uh-huh," Tess said. She listened a moment and then her eyes got big, and her mouth opened in the shape of a tiny *o*.

"What's the matter?" Roger whispered.

Tess didn't answer. Apparently, Mrs. LaMasters was still talking.

"Mrs. LaMasters?" Tess said, looking very worried. "Are you okay?"

There was another pause. Tess turned away from the boys and stared out the window.

"Okay," she said in a soft voice. "Well, tell Kara I hope she feels better. Ben and Roger do too. Bye."

Tess slowly took the receiver from her ear and hung it on the wall.

"What's wrong?" Ben asked. "What did Mrs. LaMasters say?"

"I don't know what's wrong," Tess said. "But Mrs. LaMasters was really upset. She even started *crying*."

Kara's Illness

"I've never heard a grown-up cry before," Tess said to her mother.

"Well, honey," Mrs. Munro said, "Kara's mother was probably worried about her." She glanced sideways at her daughter. "Grown-ups do cry, you know. Sometimes they just don't want their kids to see."

Tess and her mother stood side by side at the kitchen counter. Tess sliced cucumbers for a salad, and Mrs. Munro arranged chicken breasts in a flat baking dish.

Tess looked up at her mother. "I've never seen you cry," she said.

Mrs. Munro smiled. "I've cried plenty," she said.

"When you and Dad got a divorce?" Tess said.

"Yes, I cried then," her mother said. She hugged Tess. "But I'm very happy now with my two wonderful girls."

"I'm happy with you and Ashley, Mom," Tess said. "Even though Ashley's a royal pain sometimes."

Her mother laughed.

"Mrs. LaMasters said she didn't know when Kara would be coming back to school," Tess said. She sighed. "I hate it when I'm sick. I wish there were something I could do for her."

"There's a lot you can do for her," her mother said.

"What?"

"You can pray for her," Mrs. Munro said.

"Oh, yeah," Tess said. "Okay, I will." She closed her eyes. Then she opened them. "But I don't know what's wrong with her. How do I know what to pray for?"

"Well," her mother said, "you could ask for all good and healthy things for Kara. That would cover everything."

"Oh, good idea," Tess said.

She closed her eyes again and mumbled a soft prayer there over the cucumbers. Then she looked up at her mother. "Mrs.

Pilkington says you can pray anytime, so I figured now was as good a time as any."

"I agree," her mother said.

It didn't take Tess, Ben, and their classmates long to find out what was wrong with Kara.

"Boys and girls," said Ms. Conley the next morning, just after the final bell. "Let me have your attention, please. I have some news about Kara LaMasters."

Ms. Conley stood at the front of the classroom. She looked very serious, and all the kids in the room quieted down and turned their attention to their teacher.

"As you know, Kara's been absent from school all this week and a few days last week," said Ms. Conley.

Some of the kids nodded.

"Yeah, that's right," said Rebecca Holt. "Where is she?"

"Well, she's at home," Ms. Conley said. "Mrs. LaMasters called me yesterday afternoon. She said that some of Kara's classmates had called to find out how Kara was doing."

Tess and Ben looked at each other and

nodded. They knew they were the class-mates Mrs. LaMasters was talking about.

"Mrs. LaMasters asked me to explain Kara's illness to you," Ms. Conley said. "Kara went to the doctor yesterday. She gave Kara some blood tests and then sent her to the hospital for more tests."

"Is she really sick?" asked Nikki Bremer.

"Yes," said Ms. Conley. "I'm afraid that Kara's quite ill."

"What does she have?" Ben asked.

"It's called leukemia," said Ms. Conley. "It's a kind of cancer."

"Cancer?" said Rich Adams, his eyes wide. "My grandmother had cancer, and she died. Is Kara going to die?"

Ms. Conley paused a moment before she answered. "Many people with leukemia recover and live long, healthy lives."

"But some of them die?" Tess said.

Ms. Conley nodded. "Sometimes. Leukemia is a very serious illness. But we'll hold good thoughts in our minds for Kara, and we'll expect that she will get well and be back with us before too long."

"And we'll pray," Ben said.

"Absolutely," said Ms. Conley. "And if

any of you talk with Kara, be sure and talk to her as if you expect her to be well and back at school soon. We can help keep her spirits up."

"Can we call her?" asked Britt Spector.

"I think it would be wise to wait for a few days," said Ms. Conley. "Kara and her family are trying to adjust to the big news right now. But why don't we work together on a big card for Kara? Everyone can write a message telling her that we miss her and want her to get well soon."

"Great idea!" said Tess. "It can be really big, and everyone can have a page. It'll be practically a book!"

Ms. Conley smiled. "I think Kara will like that very much."

Tess smiled, too, but she felt sad. She looked at Ben. He wasn't smiling at all.

So Many Questions

"It's not fair!" Ben Brophy said. "Kara's one of the nicest kids I know."

Tess nodded. "Why did this have to happen to her?"

"How could God let Kara get leukemia?" Roger said. "How could He let something this awful happen to her?"

The kids sat on the floor of their tree house over Mrs. Pilkington's yard.

It had been a very sad day. None of the kids felt like studying, so Ms. Conley let her students work on Kara's big get-well card instead of their usual lessons. Roger's teacher had let him join the third graders, since he was a good friend of Kara's.

Tess leaned back against the tree-house

wall. "I thought God was supposed to take care of us," she said.

"He does," Ben said.

"Well, He sure isn't doing a very good job with Kara!" Tess said.

Ben nodded. "When Grandma died last year, I felt really sad, but she'd lived a long, long time. At the funeral everybody talked about what a wonderful life she'd had."

Tess and Roger nodded.

"I know everybody dies sometime," Ben said. "And I know Ms. Conley says that some people with leukemia do live. But I can't help worrying about Kara. She's not like Grandma. She's just a kid. She hasn't had a long, wonderful life yet. It's just not fair."

"Mrs. Pilkington said God wants us to give Him our problems," Roger said. "Why don't we pray for Kara? We can ask God to take care of her."

"I already did," Tess said. "In fact, I've been praying for her a lot since yesterday." She looked up at Ben and Roger, and she frowned. "Think it will do any good?"

"I sure hope so," Ben said.

"But don't you think Kara's mom and dad

have prayed for her ever since she was born?" Tess asked.

"Sure," Ben said.

"So why would God let Kara get so sick?" Tess said. "Didn't God hear their prayers? Wasn't He listening?"

Roger stood up. "I'm going to get Mrs. P.," he said. "I want to talk to her about Kara."

"I do too," said Tess. "She helped us before with that bully Brad Garth. Maybe she'll know what to do this time. Ask her to come up to the tree house, okay?"

"Sure," Roger said.

Roger stepped over to Mrs. Pilkington's garage roof and disappeared down the side. Tess and Ben stood up and watched Roger walk to Mrs. P.'s back door. Tess leaned her elbows on the edge of the tree-house wall that came up a little higher than her waist.

Roger knocked on Mrs. P.'s door. After a little while, he knocked again.

"Isn't she home?" Tess called out.

Roger turned around and looked up at them. The afternoon sun glinted off the lenses in his glasses. He shrugged. "Guess not," Roger said. "Maybe she went to her aerobics class."

Tess sighed. "I'm going home," she said, staring at the tree-house floor, her voice heavy with sadness. She put her hand on her chest. "I have an ache in here. It's been there ever since Ms. Conley told us how sick Kara is." She looked at Ben. "Do you think that's what a broken heart feels like?"

"I don't know," he said, "but I hurt in there too." He nodded towards the door. "Come on, let's go. I want to go home too."

They climbed down from the tree house.

"I'll come see Mrs. P. later," Roger said, joining them in the center of the yard. "I'll ask her if she'll be here tomorrow after school."

"I'm going to talk to my mom," Tess said.

"Me too," Ben said. "And I'm going to talk to God too."

"Well, I don't feel much like talking to Him," Tess said, wiping a tear from her eye with a swipe of her finger. "To tell you the truth, I'm pretty mad at Him right now!"

"Tess is mad at God," Ben said to his

mother. "She thinks God ought to make Kara well again."

Ben had found his mother raking the fall leaves scattered around the yard.

"I can understand how Tess feels," his mother said. "But it isn't God's fault." She stopped working and leaned on her rake. "People just get sick. God doesn't give them illness."

"Maybe He didn't make her sick," Ben said. "But why doesn't He make her well?"

"We have to be patient," she said. "Meanwhile, you're helping her with your prayers."

"You mean," Ben said, "if I pray hard enough, God won't let Kara die?"

"It doesn't work that way, honey," Mrs. Brophy said. "But whatever happens, God will be with Kara, you can be sure of that."

Ben thought a minute. Then he asked his mom, "Why does one person get sick and die and another person gets well? And both people had friends and family praying for them."

"Those are very good questions, Ben," his mother said. "I wish I had good answers for you, but I don't."

Ben felt frustrated. Usually when he wanted an answer, he could ask one of his parents or his teacher or his pastor. But so far, he wasn't getting any good answers to his questions about Kara.

"I know sometimes life doesn't seem fair," Mrs. Brophy said. "But we must trust in God, and He will take care of us. That's His promise to us."

"Do you think Pastor Sawyer would know why some people get well and some don't?" Ben asked. "He told our Sunday school class we could talk to him anytime we wanted to."

"I don't think anyone has magic answers to those questions, Ben," his mother said. "Not even pastors. People have always asked those questions, but no one can answer them for sure. But I think talking to Pastor Sawyer is a good idea. Why don't you give him a call?

"Okay," Ben said. "And maybe Tess and Roger could go with me."

"Good," his mother said. "In the meantime, why don't you grab a rake and help me for awhile? Sometimes when I have a problem, I like to work outside. It helps clear my mind a little."

"Okay," Ben said.

He headed for the garage thinking that was just what he needed: to clear his mind of all the clutter of questions about Kara. It was all too mixed up, too confusing.

Maybe Pastor Sawyer could help him straighten out the clutter.

Tess's Idea

"If you step over the line," Tess said, "I'm going to tell Mom."

"I'm so scared, I'm shaking all over," Ashley said. She stood calmly in front of the floor-length mirror, examining the new skirt she had just hemmed.

Tess sat cross-legged on her bed and leaned against her corduroy reading pillow. She scowled and kept her eye on the chalk line she had drawn across the hardwood floor of the bedroom she shared with her sister. The line divided the room exactly in half.

"You stay on your side, and I'll stay on mine," Tess said.

"Suits me fine," Ashley said. She turned to one side and then the other, examining her skirt with a critical eye. "Think this hem should be a little shorter?"

"Are you kidding?" said Tess. "It's half-way to your neck already."

Ashley rolled her eyes. "It is not! And what's bugging you? You've been mad for the last three days! Crab, crab, crab!"

"Anybody'd be crabby if they had to share a room with you, Ashley!" Tess said. "First, you're a slob. Your clothes and shoes are thrown all over the place. Second, you've got so much stuff in here, it's driving me crazy! Look at all those compact disks and makeup and . . . and pictures of boys, boys, boys! All over! Why bother with *wallpaper*, for crying out loud?"

Ashley turned to stare at Tess. "What's with you, Tess?" she said angrily. "Lately you're either moping around or yelling your head off about something."

Tess's eyes filled with tears. She put her face in her hands and took a couple of shaky breaths.

"Nothing," she said. "Just leave me alone."

"Tess," Ashley said. "Something's

wrong. You're acting weirder than usual." She paused. "Is it Kara?"

Tess lifted her head and gazed at her sister. Tears washed into her eyes, and Ashley's form became blurry. She blinked. The tears spilled down her face, and Ashley's image cleared again.

"I'm so afraid she's going to die," Tess said almost in a whisper.

Ashley walked over the chalk line and sat on Tess's bed.

"I know," she said, resting a hand on Tess's arm. "I thought that might be it. You and Kara are pretty good friends, aren't you?"

"Yeah," Tess said. "We've been friends forever."

"It's so sad," Ashley said.

"Well, why doesn't God make her well?" Tess said.

"I don't know," Ashley said.

"Why do people have to die young?" Tess said. "Kids should never have to die when they haven't even had a chance to live yet."

"I don't know that either," Ashley said.

"Nobody knows anything!" Tess cried. "That's why I'm so mad. And nobody but

God can help Kara, and He doesn't seem to care at all!"

"Oh, I'm sure God loves Kara a lot," Ashley said. "Who wouldn't love Kara? Anyway, God loves every person on earth."

The phone rang in their mother's room.

"I'll get it," Ashley said.

She hurried out of the bedroom but returned in a few minutes.

"It's for you," Ashley said. Then she lowered her voice. "I think it's Kara."

Tess gasped and scrambled off the bed. She ran down the hall and into her mother's room.

"Hello?" she said into the receiver.

"Tess?" The voice was soft. "Hi, it's Kara."

"Kara!" she cried. "How are you? *Where* are you? How are you feeling?"

She heard Kara giggle a little, but her laugh was so soft Tess could hardly hear it.

"Fine," Kara said. "Well, not really fine, I guess. I'm in the hospital right now. I've been feeling pretty sick, but I got the card from the kids at school."

"Did you like it?" Tess asked.

"Yeah," Kara said. "I love it. It's really

great. Thanks for sending it. Tell everybody I said thanks."

"Oh, sure, I will!" Tess said. She sank down onto her mother's bed.

Tess didn't say anything for a moment, not knowing quite what to say. "Does it hurt?" she said finally.

"Sometimes," Kara said. "But mostly, I feel really sick. The medicine makes me sick. And I'm really tired."

"I miss you," Tess said. "We all do. Ben misses you especially at the softball games, and Roger misses your help with the cross-word puzzles. And I . . . I just miss seeing you so much!"

"I miss you guys too," Kara said. Her voice got softer. "Boy, I wish I could be at school instead of here. I wish I felt good."

"I wish you felt good too," Tess said.

She wished she could reach through the telephone line and hug her friend. "Kara?" she said. "Could Ben and Roger and I come and see you?"

"After I get out of the hospital," Kara said. "In a week or so. I can't wait to see you guys."

"We can't wait either," Tess said. "A

week. That's such a long time. But we'll be there!"

"My mom says I need to get off the phone," Kara said. "My supper just came. I have to try and eat it."

"Okay," Tess said. "Thanks for calling, Kara."

"Bye," Kara said. "And thanks again for the card."

"Bye."

Tess hung up the phone and stared out the window next to her mother's bed.

"How's she doing?" Ashley was standing in the doorway.

"Okay," Tess said. "She sounds okay, but she's really tired. And kind of lonely."

"Yeah," Ashley said. "I'll bet she is."

The phone rang shrilly at Tess's elbow. Ashley grabbed it.

"Hello?" Ashley said. "Oh, hi, Jeff!"

She waved at Tess.

"I know, I know," Tess said, rolling her eyes. "I'm leaving."

She trudged down the hall to her room and flopped on the bed. She rolled over, put her hands behind her head, and stared at the ceiling.

It was good to hear Kara's voice. Tess was glad Kara liked the card from the kids. Tess wished there were more things she could do to cheer Kara up a little. They'd always had such fun together.

And that's when the idea came to her.

How about a memory box? Tess thought. How about giving Kara a box decorated with bright paper and ribbons? And inside she'd put dozens of little slips of paper reminding Kara of the fun things they and their friends had done since preschool. Kara could pull out one slip of paper anytime she needed a lift. It would help her feel happier for days.

Ben and Roger could help her, and they could give the box to Kara next week!

Tess smiled for the first time in three days. Maybe the memory box would help Kara feel better.

And Tess realized that she, too, felt a little better. She didn't feel quite so helpless anymore.

She got up from her mother's bed and rushed downstairs and out the front door. She couldn't wait to tell Ben about her idea!

Pastor Sawyer

Ben sat cross-legged on the floor of the tree house and chewed on the eraser of his pencil. Tess and Roger faced him in a little circle. A pile of paper slips—white, yellow, and pink—was heaped on the floor.

"One memory I'm going to write about," Ben said, picking up a yellow slip, "is when Kara caught that fly ball in our softball game with the kids from Hoover School last year. Remember? We were tied. She caught the ball, and we won the game!"

"Yeah," Tess said, grinning. "That was a great game."

"This memory box was a good idea," Roger said. "Kara will read these slips of paper and smile and smile."

"Makes me feel good to think about it," Ben said.

"Me too," Roger said. "I know one thing I'll write about. Remember when Sam Tuttle brought his pet hamster to school, and after school it got away from him in the hall?"

"Yeah!" Tess said, laughing. "And all the kids were screaming. It was running around their feet like crazy!"

"I thought for sure someone would step on it and squish it," Ben said. "Everyone was trying to catch it."

"Until Sam yelled, 'Everybody stop!' " Roger said. "And every kid froze right on the spot. The hamster ran over to Kara and climbed up on her shoe."

"Yeah," Ben said. "And Kara calmly reached down and picked it up and handed it to Sam."

"That memory will make her laugh," Roger said.

"Good," Ben said. "Dad says laughing is good for the body and soul."

"Listen to the first memory I wrote about," Tess said. She held up her slip of pink paper and read.

WHEN EVERYBODY
WAS MAD AT MOLLY
BECAUSE WE THOUGHT
SHE'D TAKEN
LAURIE'S RING
YOU WERE THE ONLY
PERSON WHO WAS NICE TO
HER. THEN LAURIE
FOUND THE RING AT
HOME IN HER ROOM.
SHE'D FORGOTTEN
THAT SHE HADN'T EVEN
BROUGHT IT TO SCHOOL

"Yeah," Ben said. "Kara was the only person who defended Molly."

"Kara's such a good person," Tess said. She stared up into the branches over their heads. "It just isn't fair."

"No," said Ben. "It's not."

"I was feeling really sad last night because of Kara," Roger said, "so I went over to see Mrs. Pilkington. But she still wasn't there. Then my mom told me she's on vacation. She won't be back for a few days."

"Mrs. Pilkington doesn't know why Kara has to have cancer," Tess said glumly. "Nobody does!"

"Except God," Ben said.

"And He's not talking," Tess said.

"I called Pastor Sawyer," Ben said. "I'm going to see him tomorrow after school."

"To talk about Kara?" Tess said.

"Yeah," Ben said. "Do you guys want to come with me?"

"I do," Tess said. "I like his kids' sermons. He's a nice man." She frowned. "Do you think he will know why Kara got leukemia? And why God doesn't make her well?"

"I don't know," Ben said. "But I want to ask him anyway."

"I want to come too," Roger said.

"Good," Ben said. "Let's meet after school right outside the front door. We'll walk to the church together."

"Great," Tess said. "If anybody should know how to get God to make Kara well, it would be Pastor Sawyer!"

"I sure hope so," Ben said.

"Maybe now we're getting somewhere!" Tess said.

The three friends met after school the next day and walked to the church.

"You'll like Pastor Sawyer," Tess whispered to Roger after they'd pulled open the side door to the church. "He's nice, and he likes kids."

Roger nodded. "I like my church's pastor too. But we haven't lived in Brookdale very long, and I don't know him very well."

"So you can borrow our pastor," Tess said.

Ben, Tess, and Roger climbed the stairs to the second floor.

They found Pastor Sawyer sitting at his desk behind a pile of papers. He looked up and smiled when the kids walked in.

"Hi, Pastor Sawyer," Ben said. "Here we are." He pointed at Tess. "You already know Tess. And this," he said, pointing at Roger, "is Roger Quinn. He's a friend of Kara's too."

"Hi, Tess. Hi, Roger," Pastor Sawyer said. He got up from his desk and walked around to shake hands with each of the kids. Then he nodded to some chairs on the other side of his desk. "Let's sit down," he said.

The chairs were arranged in a small circle so they could all face one another.

Pastor Sawyer asked them how school was going, and then he asked Roger how his parents liked living in Brookdale. They talked a little while, and then Pastor Sawyer cleared his throat.

"Ben told me a little about why you wanted to see me," Pastor Sawyer said. "I understand you have a friend who's ill."

"Yeah," Tess said, relieved they were finally talking about Kara. "And I just don't understand it, Pastor! How come a nice girl

like Kara has to get a horrible disease like leukemia?"

"That's a tough question, Tess," Pastor Sawyer said. "I'm afraid I can't answer it for you."

Tess rolled her eyes. "It's hopeless," she said. "Nobody knows!"

"If I could answer that question," Pastor Sawyer said with a little smile, "I'd be the smartest person in the world."

"But it's not fair!" she said. "Kara's practically the nicest person I know!"

"God doesn't want bad things to happen to Kara or to any of us, Tess," the pastor said. "He doesn't give people an illness or punish them by making them sick. God wants only good for Kara."

"So why doesn't He make the bad stuff go away?" Roger said.

"Yeah," Ben said. "We've been praying and praying!"

"Doesn't He want to help?" Tess asked.

"Well," Pastor Sawyer said, "prayer doesn't work like a vending machine, where you put in a quarter and get what you want."

"But," Tess said, "He helped us with Brad Garth!"

"Brad Garth?" the pastor said.

"Yeah," Tess explained. "He's this bully at school, see, and he was beating up on kids, so we asked God to help us."

"And we know He helped us, 'cause things got better," said Roger. "I mean, Brad Garth's not exactly a sweetie pie, but he's not so bad anymore, and we can stand him now."

"Yeah," said Ben. "And Mrs. Pilkington says that God wants us to give our problems to Him."

"He does," said Pastor Sawyer. "Mrs. Pilkington is right."

"Well, we've done that!" said Tess. "We've all talked to God about Kara and given that problem to Him. But Kara's still sick!"

"Well," the pastor said, "there are some mysteries we can't explain. But I want you all to know one very important thing: God loves your friend Kara very much. He's with her, and He's watching over her. He'll be there with her no matter what happens.

God says, 'I will not leave you comfortless.' "

"God is comforting Kara?" Tess asked.

"You can be sure He is," said the pastor.

"How can you tell?" Roger asked.

"Well, one way He's comforting Kara is through you three kids," Pastor Sawyer said.

"Really?" Ben said.

"Of course!" Pastor Sawyer said. "Ben, didn't you tell me that your class made a big card for Kara?"

"Yeah," Ben said. "She really liked it."

"Well, see?" the pastor said. "Whenever you do something good for someone else—comfort someone who is sick, help someone who is needy, visit someone who is lonely—you're doing God's work. Jesus taught us that. God works through doctors, nurses, teachers, pastors, family, and friends to give comfort to people who are suffering."

Ben told the pastor about the memory box.

"Do you think God wants us to make it for her?" he asked.

"I'm sure He does, Ben," Pastor Sawyer said. "And your prayers help Kara too." He paused a moment before he spoke again. "Prayers are powerful. They tell God how much you love Kara."

"Okay," Tess said. "We'll keep on praying for her."

"I think," said Pastor Sawyer, "that instead of asking ourselves why bad things happen, we should ask ourselves how God can use us to help others in need."

"Yeah," said Tess. "I see what you mean. We can't answer the 'why?' question anyway."

"That's right," said the pastor. "And continue to pray for Kara. We'll pray for her this afternoon before you leave. And be patient."

Tess sighed loudly. "I'll try."

"Patience isn't one of Tess's strong points, Pastor Sawyer," Ben said.

The pastor laughed. "We can probably all improve in that area," he said.

"Even you?" Tess said.

"Even me," said Pastor Sawyer.

Tess grinned. She was looking at Ben and Roger and smiling too.

She was glad they had come to talk to Pastor Sawyer. She guessed he was right.

No one could answer the big "why?" question about Kara's illness. But maybe she and Ben and Roger could help God give Kara comfort and love.

That made her feel good—to think she could be one of God's helpers.

And she couldn't wait to give Kara the box filled with memories.

6

A Visit with Kara

"I'm kind of nervous," Tess said.

"Me too," Ben said.

"Me three," said Roger.

"My mom said Kara might not have much hair," Tess said. "The medicine for cancer can make your hair fall out."

The kids walked down the sidewalk toward Kara's house. Tess clutched the memory box, which she had wrapped in pink and blue paper and tied with a dark pink ribbon.

She looked at Ben. "Do you think Kara will be bald?"

Ben shrugged. "I don't know."

"I'm glad she finally called," Tess said. "I thought she'd never call us to come over! What's it been—nearly three weeks?"

"Yeah," Roger said. "Two weeks and five days to be exact."

The kids rounded the corner, and the LaMasters' house came into view. It was a white, two-story house with a small, neat yard.

"Her room is upstairs," Tess said, pointing.

The shades were up, and the window was open a little to let in a fresh breeze.

The kids approached the front door and knocked. After a few seconds, Mrs. La-Masters opened the door and smiled at the three visitors.

"Hi, Tess," she said. "Come on in."

Tess felt relieved. Mrs. LaMasters looked much happier than she'd sounded on the phone three weeks ago. Tess was sure she wasn't going to cry today.

"Hi, Mrs. LaMasters," Tess said. "This is Ben Brophy, and that's Roger Quinn."

"Hello, boys," Mrs. LaMasters said.

She moved back, and the three kids stepped inside.

"Go right on up," Mrs. LaMasters said. "Kara's resting in her room."

Tess, Ben, and Roger trooped up the stairs and down the hall to Kara's bedroom.

Tess peeked into the room first. Her heart was beating hard. She didn't know how Kara would look.

And Tess didn't know how she would act if Kara looked awful.

But she wanted so much to let Kara know how much she was missed—and loved.

"Kara?" she said softly.

Kara was stretched out on her bed in her nightgown and robe, reading a book. When she heard Tess's voice, she closed the book.

"Hi," she said, lifting her head. "Come on in."

The three kids moved into the room.

A purple scarf was wrapped around Kara's head and tied behind her neck.

"Hi, Kara," Tess said.

Tess relaxed immediately. Kara looked thin and tired, but she smiled and looked happy to see them. Kara was still Kara, her good friend.

"Hi, Kara," Ben said.

"Hi, Kara," Roger said.

"Hi," Kara answered. She sat up and

leaned against her pillow. "Gee, it's good to see you guys."

Tess sat down on the bed next to Kara. She wanted to hug her but felt a little shy.

"How are you feeling?" Tess said.

"Better," Kara said. "I'm not taking the medicine now that made me so sick."

"Great!" Tess said.

"Yeah," Roger said. "You look pretty good, Kara."

"Yeah, you do," Ben said.

Kara beamed. "Thanks," she said. She patted the scarf on her head. "Mom says maybe I'll start a new fashion craze with this scarf." She paused a moment. "The doctors say my hair will grow back before I know it."

"Sure," Tess said. "Hair grows fast, and your hair was short to begin with."

"Yeah," Kara said. "So what's new at school?"

"Same old stuff," Ben said. "Everybody can't wait to have you back, Kara."

"Dr. McDonald says maybe another couple of weeks," Kara said. "If everything goes okay."

"Fabulous!" cried Tess. "I was afraid . . ." She stopped herself.

Kara looked at her curiously. "You were afraid of what?"

Tess felt her cheeks get hot. She'd almost blurted out something horrible.

"You mean, that I might die?" Kara said.

"Oh, I didn't mean . . ." Tess started to say. "Oh, I'm sorry. I'm really sorry."

"No, that's okay," Kara said. "I'm doing a lot better now. Dr. McDonald says now we wait to see how it goes." She smiled a little. "I was afraid for awhile too."

"Yeah," Tess said softly. "I would've been afraid if I were you."

"But I'm not afraid anymore," Kara said.

"Because you're feeling better?" Tess said.

"Well, that's part of it," Kara said. "But it's . . . it's . . . something else too."

With her finger, Kara thoughtfully traced over a blue flower on her bedspread. She looked up.

"It's kind of hard to put into words," she said. "But I know . . . I mean, I really *know* that God's with me. Everything changed when He told me that."

"He told you?" Tess said. Her eyes were big.

"Well, not in English," Kara said. "I mean, not in exact words. He just let me know He was here. That was when I was really scared. And really, really sick. And from then on, I wasn't afraid anymore."

She paused a moment. "You know," she said, "in church we talk about Jesus dying on the cross for us, but now I really understand why God sent Jesus to us. So we won't have to be afraid to die, and we can know how much He loves us."

There was a short silence in the room. "That's great," Ben said, his voice barely above a whisper.

"Yeah," Tess said.

"I don't want to die," Kara said. "But when I do die someday, I won't be afraid, because I know that God will be with me. And He will take me home with Him to heaven."

Kara smiled, and Tess stared back at her friend. There was something very special in Kara's eyes, something new, something calm and peaceful, that made Tess feel good all over.

Kara glanced down at the package in Tess's hands. She grinned.

"So are you going to give me the present or not?" she said.

"Oh, I forgot!" Tess cried.

Kara laughed, and so did Tess, Ben, and Roger.

"I've been trying to be polite since you got here," Kara said. "But I can't wait to see what it is!"

"Here!" Tess said, thrusting it into Kara's hands. "Ben, Roger, and I made it for you."

Kara unwrapped the package and turned the box over in her hands. "This is great," she said.

Tess laughed. "No, silly. That's just the box! It's what's inside that's important."

Kara laughed and opened the box filled with colorful slips of paper.

"Pull out one of the papers," Tess said. "Just one. And read it."

Kara pulled a yellow slip out of the box. She held it up and began to read.

"One day when I was really sad, you cheered me up by telling me funny jokes. That's when I realized what a great friend you were."

"Remember that?" Ben said. "Last year

after I struck out in our game against the Wilson team? And we lost the game?"

Kara smiled. "Yeah," she said. "I remember."

"You were great," Ben said.

Kara smiled shyly, and then she shrugged. "What are friends for?"

Tess reached out finally and hugged Kara. "That box is full of memories," she said. "Pull one out every day."

"Only one?" Kara said. "Are you kidding? I'm going to read them all as soon as you guys leave!"

The kids laughed.

Tess looked at Kara, then at Ben and Roger, all of them laughing. She thought of how nervous she had been to come here. But she couldn't remember ever feeling surrounded by so much . . . well, it had to be love, she thought. It felt so wonderful.

The kids had been praying for Kara to be healed. Whether or not she was going to have good health was something they would have to wait for.

But Kara had, without a doubt, been touched in some special way by God. She had a new light in her eyes, a new spirit of love for God.

And she wasn't afraid anymore.

"Thank you, God," Tess said softly. She felt love and happiness fill her completely. "You *were* with Kara all along, weren't You?"